A · LIFE ·
KNOWLE

1902 – 1986

Gladys · Plaster

White Tree
Books

First published in 1987 by
WHITE TREE BOOKS,
an imprint of REDCLIFFE PRESS LTD,
49 Park Street, Bristol BS1 5NT

Dedicated
to my great-grand-daughter
Laura Frances Goodacre

ISBN 0 948265 71 X

Typeset and printed by
WBC Print Ltd, Bristol

CONTENTS

MOVING IN

With nostalgia I look back so many years to the Knowle I knew when I was young, a Knowle free from the noise of heavy lorries belching out diesel fumes, hardly a motor car to be seen, no traffic lights, no pedestrian crossings, no noisy transistors, just the plodding of the horses carrying their loads up and down the hill, and the electric trams, always available. We knew no other world. On a market day, the sheep would be driven slowly along, holding up what traffic happened to be in the way, as they patiently wended their way down through Bushy Park and the Three Lamps, making for Cattle Market Road. Riding a bike was quite safe, but one had to be wary of the tram lines.

My parents, together with their four children, came to Bristol from Derby in 1902. My father, on the staff of the old Midland Railway, had been transferred to the District Manager's Office in Corn Street, where he was made Chief Staff Clerk.

They chose to make their new home in Knowle, as it appeared to be a beautiful suburb, set high on a hill, and practically surrounded with lovely green fields, and wild flowers growing in abundance, which is a rare sight in these modern days. The main Wells Road, planted with young saplings, gave promise of leafy trees overhanging the elegant houses which lined the road. There were plenty of shops, and Temple Meads Station was within easy walking distance. On a fine morning commuters would enjoy a brisk walk into the City, ignoring the trams although for just two old pennies one could ride right into the Knowle tram stop at Bristol Bridge. Unfortunately when the weather was wet, one would have no shelter on top of the trams, but the seats were movable, enabling one to turn the wet one by just folding the seat over. Of course, the tram drivers were not so well protected from the elements, but they wore heavy leather gloves and stout uniforms. The well protected 'bus drivers of to-day would not appreciate that sort of job, especially having to stand up whilst driving.

My family's first home was in Harrowdene Road, close to the recently built Wells Road Schools, and handy for the shops on the Wells Road, also for the Triangle shops. Some houses were then not built, and there was still grassland, it being part of the Knowle Farm Estate.

Mother did not really care for her new abode. She was nervous about the narrow lane at the back of the house, dividing

Harrowdene Road from the houses in Maxse Road. Maxse Road was named after Lady Maxse who owned part of the land. My eldest sister succumbed to the dreadful diptheria which was then rampant in Bristol, necessitating her removal to Ham Green Hospital, and then my eldest brother fell ill with scarlet fever – another patient for Ham Green. Mother decided enough was enough, and they moved to No. 4, Cleeve Road, just near, where I was born in 1905. Before moving, another sister had been born, and mother was able to watch as she lay in bed nine dedicated gentlemen lay a foundation stone, each intended for the building of Harrowdene United Methodist Church. The decision to "erect a building in which to preach the unsearchable riches of Christ, and to train children in the fear of God" was made at a meeting of local Bible Christians on October 1st, 1902. The School premises were completed first, and the Sunday School was started on February 5th, 1905, along with Junior and Senior Christian Endeavour Societies. The official opening of the Church (to seat 550 worshippers) took place on May 30th, 1906. On December 20th, the Church had one of its "high days", when Madam Clara Butt (at one time a scholar at the Redcliffe Crescent Sunday School, now sadly extinct as a result of the last War) and her husband Mr. Kennerly Rumford, sang at a sacred concert in the church. One of Madam Clara Butt's solos was "Abide with Me", in which she was accompanied by the composer, Samuel Liddle.

How we enjoyed our leisure hours in those early days, playing hopscotch, pottle, skipping, bowling hoops – the boys had iron ones, noisy things, and we whipped our gaily coloured tops. We blew bubbles with the aid of soapy water and clay pipes, but then skating began to be all the rage, and we hoped for the best. Yes! we were lucky.

When Father took my sister Chrissie and me down to Smith's Ironmongers shop on the Wells Road, next door to Alan Ball, the Chemist, and also next door to the Post Office, we could only obtain one pair, which had leather at the back of the heel, so being the elder, Chrissie had those, whilst I had to curb my impatience until the arrival of more skates. Incidentally Smith's shop afterwards took over Chard's shop, which was on the opposite side of the road, and finally finishing up with a very fine store at the corner of the Wells Road and Broad Walk, which, of course was not in existence in my very young days, it being part of the old Race Course, followed by the Golf Links.

We always kept our skates well oiled, to give more speed when racing each other. We all felt very envious when Winnie Cowley from No. 21, Cleeve, displayed her pair of ball bearings. Ours paled to insignificance against hers, but she had to be very cautious when

6

using them, as they would go very fast. One incident will always stay in my memory. Skating down Marston Road, in the middle, as pavements were then forbidden for skating, my speed rapidly increased, the road sloping quite considerably towards the Wells Road. I frantically tried to stop, a feat which I had never mastered, and desperately hoping there would be no traffic coming along, over I went at high speed, finishing up against the kerb on the opposite side of the road. Phew! What an escape! Just suppose that had

happened in these modern times! It does not bear thinking about.

Stephen's Fields, later termed St. Martin's Fields, were a favourite rendezvous – a fine place to take our dolls' sewing and drink a bottle of lemonade. From the brow of the hill one could watch the train puffing its way from Brislington Station on towards Temple Meads Station, and behind the tall trees at the bottom of the fields one could see the Imperial Grounds and Pavilion. Tobogganning all the way down the steep hill was much enjoyed when there happened to be a heavy fall of snow, but enthusiasm was afterwards damped when a Mrs. Hopkins who lived in Jubilee Road crashed at the bottom and broke her leg.

Dingley Dell – what memories are recalled! Sliding down the steep muddy banks to the bottom, or paddling and fishing for tiddlers in the pond below. How our mothers deplored the state of our clothes invariably covered with red mud!

————— STREET TRADERS —————

Clambering on to Frank Stephens' milk float when it arrived in our road was another highlight, but I doubt if his old horse enjoyed pulling the extra weight of cheering kids. Stephens were well known as long established farmers, and they also kept the dairy in Greenmore Road. Greenmore's name was derived by the linking of Alderman Frank Moore's name and Mr. Greenough, a land owner who also owned the drapery shop at the corner of Cheapside and the Wells Road, Totterdown. Frank Moore lived in Knowle House, on the corner of Priory and Talbot Roads. The grounds were quite extensive, but now new houses occupy the site. Anyone wishing to purchase milk at the dairy would take their jugs to the front door, giving a hearty pull at the rope attached to the door bell, and then a little window would open on the inside door, and in my young days, old Mrs. Stephens would answer it.

Then there was the arrival of the barrel organ man and his wife, who wore a gaily coloured head scarf, and their donkey. After their repertoire outside No. 3, Cleeve Road, where they always stopped, out would emerge holding a paper bag of titbits old Mr. Barber, who had very white hair and a beard. The donkey was always ready for his treat. Mr. Barber's sister was very partial to cats. We never knew how many she owned.

Mr. Boughtwood who owned the off licence on the corner of Redcatch Lane created much interest when he trundled his barrow laden with bottles up our road. Then we would carefully watch to see

at which houses he called. In our opinion, these were the secret drinkers. We had learned about the dangers of strong drink as Band of Hope members, when we used to roar out with great gusto, "Merry Dick you all must know, for he lives in Jackson's Row". We had no knowledge of Merry Dick, but we knew his drink was "water bright, from the crystal spring".

Often when we were having our meals, our back gate would open, and a very tall figure would come into view, having a large basket perched on top of her head. She would knock on the back door, and

9

Mother would at once rummage for her purse. The "Old Lady" had arrived. Mother would inspect her wares, and always purchase something, knots of tape, needles, packets of pins, and what have you. Then the basket was once again placed on top of her head, and the "Old Lady" would make a stately departure. We never knew her name, or from where she came.

Mother never refused to buy pegs, etc., from a gypsy, for fear of promoting bad luck. She was very superstitious, always crossing her fingers when walking under a ladder, if she spilled salt, she would immediately throw some over her left shoulder in memory of Lot's wife who made the mistake of looking over her shoulder, and was turned into a pillar of salt. Two knives crossed was the sign of a quarrel, and one must never open up an umbrella in the house. That would cause very bad luck!

Mr. Matthews was Stephen's Milk delivery man. He would carry his heavy can up the entry, and measure out the required milk into the waiting jugs. In my dinner hour I often trotted down Greenmore Road to Sage's bakery, the first shop in Redcatch Road. Mr. Sage's name can still be seen marked out in the stonework over the shop which is now a Chinese chip shop. Sometimes I would just buy yeast so that Mother could make a batch of teacakes. Apparently on one occasion when I was just a toddler some yeast disappeared from the kitchen table, and it was always assumed I had eaten it. The very thought of eating yeast makes me feel sick! Perhaps a cat ate it!

───────── LOCAL SHOPS ─────────

Queueing for food during the war turned out to be a good thing. Previously everyone pushed and shoved either to board a tram, or to get served first in a shop, but now everybody automatically queues, which is the fairest way. As children we were often pushed back, losing our turn.

We had some very good shops. Edmonds' shop was one of the most interesting, and they sold practically everything, from toys to bicycles. They also repaired the 'bikes, and would mend umbrellas. I believe this was Mr. Hallett's department. He married Lily Edmonds who also served in the shop when they had a rush of customers, generally at Christmas time.

Mother was a Co-op member. The dividend was a great help when she needed to restock our sheets and pillowcases. A number of Knowle residents scorned to patronise the Co-op, especially the ones who lived in the large houses in St. Martin's Road and on the Wells

Road. Rudman's high class grocery store was the recipient of their favours. Nell and Mabel Windmill who kept the sweet shop next door to Rudmans were great favourites with everyone. After playing tennis, most Knowlites sat at the tables in the little room leading off from the shop, partaking of a dish of their delicious ice cream. Why does the modern ice cream taste so different, and not nearly so good? We all loved watching the pair of lovebirds kept in a cage in the little room, they always seemed to be billing and cooing.

As for Mr. Chard, the ironmonger, we always wondered if he spent his spare time partaking of light refreshment at the neighbouring Talbot Hotel. His nose was certainly very red!

Mother frequently took us for a walk down to Bushy Park. She was very friendly with Mr. Tozer and the Harris family. Mary Harris attended Wells Road School when I was there, and her young brother took over the shop when his parents died. Now Totterdown is in process of being restored, although perhaps not to its former glory.

Father often liked to take us for long walks around West Town

Lane, especially at lambing time. We loved to watch the lambs gambolling about, and always stopped to look at the ducks swimming under the little bridge by the Imperial Ground. Talbot Lane was the worst part of our walk. Passing Brislington Station on the left and Eagle House on the right we would tackle steep and narrow Talbot Lane, lined with hedgerows, and peer at the cottages on the right, halfway up the hill. Once we walked, there and back, to Dundry. We sat on the steps which led up to the Church, and ate apples. I know I was worn out, and we still had to walk back. There was no transport in those days. I do not know how we managed to arrive at Bushy Park, as this seemed to be in quite a wrong direction. Father mistook the right road, so aware of our reproachful eyes, we boarded a tram up to Knowle.

Hygiene did not appear to be a predominating feature years ago, and it was not surprising that disease spread rapidly. The toilets in the Infants' School playground were terribly smelly as there were no water flushes, so we constantly avoided using them.

The open dust carts attracted numerous flies and other insects. The smell was really obnoxious, from all the rotting material tipped on to the carts. Occasionally the water cart came along, sprinkling water on to the dusty roads in order to lay the dust and clean them up. There was a water stand pipe at the end of Beaconsfield Road, to which the hoses were attached. Horses of course did not add to the cleanliness of the thoroughfares, but there was usually an influx of small boys eager to shovel up the manure into their buckets, selling the result of their labour to keen gardeners.

Inoculations for children against diptheria, measles, scarlet fever and whooping cough were practically non existent, and with many of the older and poorer houses lacking good sanitation, especially with the seemingly large families, health was often undermined. Knowle, of course, was not so congested as Totterdown with its hundreds of small houses crammed very closely together. Our only poorer type cottages were the ones at the Terminus, by the Red Lion Hill, obviously built for farm labourers who worked on the neighbouring farms. I could never understand why they had practically no back gardens – just a very small yard, yet there were then fields all around them. I well remember Sinnegar's grocery shop at the end of the rank – Edith Sinnegar was in my class at Wells Road. Then there were the Venns – very popular with most of us. Ernest Venn was also once in the same class as I was. He became a coal merchant, but died quite a long time ago. His brother, the milkman had a disastrous loss when the 'plane carrying so many Shepton Mallet and Axbridge families, together with his own wife, daughter, grandaughter and son-in-law crashed over Switzerland.

Their grave is just inside the Arnos Vale Cemetery, top gates. It is beautifully tended by Mr. Venn, a mass of flowers in the summer months. When I once met him there, he told me he visited the grave every day.

Tuberculosis was rampant not so very many years ago, and many factory workers contracted the disease. The Smith family living in Somerset Road lost two daughters Bernice and later on, Edna – both lovely girls, and old Mrs. Knee, a real character, living in Harrowdene Road, lost Daisy, her grandaughter.

Shop assistants had to work long hours, with poor pay. No Sunday trading was allowed, so at least they were able to enjoy a rest on those days. Even our doctors were on constant call at all hours of the day and night. When I was a child we seemed to have quite a large number of them – Dr. Robertson, Dr. Lucas, Dr. James on the corner of Beaconsfield Road, Dr. Fleming, Dr. Evans, very much loved and missed when he died, old Dr. Gawn, followed by his son, Douglas, who has also recently passed away. Dr. Hunt took over Dr. Lucas's practice, moving to the opposite side of the George Hill, and afterwards moving to a house on the Wells Road near Beaconsfield Road. Everybody was saddened by the death of his sister, Dr. Easby, who lived by the Holy Nativity Church. She suffered a great loss in losing her little son, when he drowned in their garden fish pool.

One good thing about the old days was having groceries and bread, also fruit, vegetables and fish delivered. There was no need then for shopping trolleys. Paper boys would yell out in strident voices, eager to sell their papers. The baker would take his basket of bread to each customer, so that a choice could be made. In later years, my daughter, when quite young, always made a point of fondling Kitty, Blake's horse, and giving him a titbit. If no one apparently seemed to be watching, Kitty would often mount the pavement, in order to nibble at a nearby hedge.

Father often walked down Greenmore Road to buy his evening paper from the person – he called her the "Old Lady", but she was weather beaten, and looked older than she really was – who always stood outside Wakefield's sweet shop.

We were lucky in having a side entrance to our house when the coal man called – he was able to open the back gate in order to deliver the coal, but some people were unfortunate in having to have theirs delivered via the front door.

The top of the lime kiln, where the Gaiety Cinema stands, was a favourite look-out place, giving us all a marvellous view of the cricket in progress in the cricket field. The bowling green was not so attractive. Watching elderly men walking backwards and forwards bowling bowls seemed to us just a grown up way of playing marbles. The tennis courts were more interesting, where there was plenty of activity. There were three tennis clubs. "Firfield" was for the more elite and skilful players. "The Avenue" was favoured mostly by the teaching fraternity. The "Knowle" is still flourishing, and there was one private court owned by the Brookhouse Richards family. They lived on the Wells Road, and Mr. Brookhouse Richards was eventually Lord Mayor of Bristol. My three sisters and I first of all joined the Y.M.C.A. Club, now replaced by Tennis Road. Later, my three sisters joined the "Avenue", whilst I went farther afield as far as the St. Mary Redcliffe Playing Field, which was reached by hopping over the stile at the bottom of Redcatch Lane, crossing a couple of fields, not far from Eagle Farm. I played tennis in the summer, and hockey in the winter months. Veering to the right before reaching the grounds one could arrive at the Novers Fever Hospital. Merrywood Boys School now occupies part of the Redcliffe Grounds.

14

There were no houses on one side of the George Hill, just the ruins of either an old farmhouse or cottage. In his Journal for October 15th, 1759, John Wesley, the famous preacher, relates: "I walked up to Knowle, a mile from Bristol to see the French prisoners. About eleven hundred of them, we were informed, were confined in that little place, without anything to lie upon but a little dirty straw, or anything to cover them but a few foul rags, either by day or night, so that they died like rotten sheep". It would be interesting to know whether those ruins on the hill were any connection with that "little place". At the start of the summer vacation, my best friend, Kitty Belsten and I used to climb up by the ruins, eagerly watching for the first sight of our brothers and their friends arriving at Bushy Park, dressed in their City School clothes. The school only catered for boarders in those days. The usual holiday meeting place was on our long entry wall at the side of our house. There we would make plans for our activities, quite often involving chasings all around Knowle.

I still remember clutching hold of my mother's hand as we went along Maxse Road, for my first day in Wells Road Infants School. I was upset when after taking a seat at the front of the classroom, I was pushed away from the desk by a boy, claiming I had taken his seat. Not a very good start! Then when books were handed round, I was really worried – all the class seemed to be abe to read, except me. How and when I eventually learned is not in my retentive memory, but I do remember being moved up to what was termed the Big School. Miss Passmore, the Infants' Headmistress wore spectacles, and a very high necked blouse. Her skirt reached to her ankles. I always thought, and I still think the same now, that fashions in my young days were absolutely ridiculous, long skirts dragging the ground, picking up all the grime from the roads. Children's clothes were definitely ugly – at least I thought so. Their dresses were practically down to their ankles, black woollen stockings – mine were always well darned at the knees due to my tendency to fall down when running too fast. We often wore white pinafores, and button or lace-up boots. What I detested most was the awful combinations we had to wear even when we were older, a relic of the Victorian days, I suspect. These were never discarded even on the hottest of days. Looking at the way modern children are dressed, with plenty of air reaching their limbs, I realise I had good reason for my grievances.

My first impressions of the Big School were very mixed. There seemed to be a different atmosphere altogether. Mr. Edwards, the

Headmaster was very awe inspiring. He strode about, wearing a black gown, and nearly always carrying a cane. Woe betide any culprit standing by his desk in the hall, awaiting inevitable punishment. The discipline in those days was very strict, no chatting when moving between classrooms, and definitely no chatting amongst ourselves in class. We were well drilled in the three Rs. Permission to use the locked lavatories under the shed in the playground was obtained by raising up one's hand and asking for the key. I found this all very embarrassing, and one was apt to hang on as long as possible until playtime break, or until it was time to go home. Of course there were no school dinners. Our mothers were "Stay-At-Home" Mothers, nearly always there when we arrived home. How different from to-day, when so many children have to go home to an empty home, waiting for their mothers to arrive from work.

The large playground was divided by iron railings, separating the boys from the girls and infants. However, the railings did not deter the girls chatting to the boys whilst having our lunch. I was horrified when one of the boys whom I liked told me he was eating bread and lard. Another boy always seemed well supplied with sweets – every day he would call me over and give me a sweet.

When the whistle blew at the end of playtime, we would all make a rush to get on to our lines. We were taking no chances!

We generally felt very bored when we had to learn a new song. The Tonic Sol Fa would be chalked out on the blackboard, and it was a case of watching the pointer and reading the notes. We knew all the old favourites, such as "John Peel", "Barbara Allen", and "Sweet Lass of Richmond Hill", but when it came to learning: "Oh! Who will o'er the Downs with me, oh! Who will with me ride", I used to think it was time for the bridegroom to fetch his "blooming bride" himself, and not ask for someone to help him! The tune was really monotonous.

On Empire Day we all assembled in the Hall, in order to have a service, and sing "Flag of Britain".

Miss Edwards decided to celebrate May Day, by letting us all vote for a May Queen. It made me think of the poem: "For I'm to be queen of the May, Mother". Never for one moment did I hold out any chance of being elected, and I have no idea for whom I voted, but I had a pleasant shock when I had drawn the same number of votes as another girl, Dorothy Loxton, who was a relative newcomer to the school. She was quite pretty, with long black ringlets, whereas I was quite mediocre, to my way of thinking. We both had to go outside into the hall, whilst the class re-voted, and this time, Dorothy won. She was to be May Queen, and I was to be her Maid of Honour, which quite satisfied me. We held the crowning ceremony in one of the fields just beyond the Red Lion Hill. Dorothy was duly crowned with May blossom, whilst I carried a bunch of flowers. We had no maypole, so proceeded to dance around the Queen.

We always dreaded the appearance of Mr. Edwards when he chose to enter our respective classes. I shall never forget how well we were drilled in inverted commas, apostrophes, full stops and semi colons. The present generation seem to blithely ignore all these rules – in fact I am continually pointing out her lack of apostrophes to my daughter when she writes. She airily dismisses them, in spite of her Red Maids' education. If ever one of the family made a mistake in grammar when writing to brother Stenson when he was at the City School, the fault would always be alluded to when he next wrote.

When reading examination time came along, we each had to walk out and stand by Mr. Edward's chair, and then read a passage. I was never nervous then, knowing I was proficient at reading, but when I once heard him give my mark to Miss McSweeney, "Fairly Good" whilst others had had "Very Good" or just "Good", I was really

17

upset. That has stayed in my memory all these years!

Sister Dorothy also had a grievance which she never forgot. Mr. Edwards held her up in front of the class, because of her good work, and all the time she was conscious her bright pink frilly knickers were on view to the whole of the class, as he had hitched up her frock when lifting her up.

Descending the steep spiral steps leading down to the Woodwork and Housewifery Rooms never appealed to me. Mr. Trump taught woodwork to the boys, but I have no recollection of the person who took the girls for housewifery. I hated the strong smell of carbolic soap, used for scrubbing down the tables. We had to learn how to make a bed, dress a baby doll, and I remember we made some oatmeal scones, which I heartily disliked when eating one. One day I slipped on the bottom step of the spiral staircase, and passed out. I presume I had given myself a shock. Mother was quite used to my passing out, as I called it. Once I slipped as she tried to lift me out of the big bath upstairs, banging my tummy on the side of the bath. She was so frightened, that she sent Chrissie to fetch Mrs. Harvey, a retired nurse, living on the corner of Selworthy Road. Mother thought quite a lot of her capabilities, and always asked her for advice over health matters.

————————SCHOOL PRIZES————————

I suppose I did reasonably well in my lessons, but I was never brilliant at arithmetic, not upholding my family's pet subject. It was always at the back of my mind when I looked at the names of my brothers and sisters printed in gold letters on the huge Honours Board in the hall that my name would never be added. I do remember, when in Miss Neale's class which was Standard Three, my eldest brother Stenson one day taught me the rudiments of H.C.Fs., and L.C.Ms. That personal teaching restored my confidence, and by the time came for the class to learn those particular sums, I astonished my teacher by always getting my sums right. Alas! I had that one time of glory only, because on reaching Standard Four I was still puzzling over my sums, but I was good at composition. I revelled in drawing and painting—that was my speciality, and from a very early age I would spend hours with a pencil and a piece of paper. My mother was quite proud of my efforts, and the results of my handiwork were invariably pinned up on the wall of our sitting room, leaving pin marks on the wallpaper on their removal. I at one time was keen on drawing a cart filled with people but, unable to draw a whole horse, I just drew the rear end with a tail. This obsession sprang from when I went for a ride in my Grandma's pony trap, in a place called Long Eaton, my mother's old home. It was situated between Derby and Nottingham. However, I managed to win two prizes before I left the school. Miss Harvey, in charge of needlework (she always had sewing materials dangling from her waist) offered a prize for the best needlework. Some of us were learning knitting and I knitted a long white vest for myself in two plain, two purl stitch. After it was finished, I took it home to show Mother. Her reaction to my piece of work was rather mixed. The knitting was very good, but, to use her expression, "it was as black as the fire back". I think that must have been one of her numerous Midlands' remarks. Anyhow, she washed it, and the result was remarkable, in fact, so different in colour that Miss Harvey awarded me the prize – Hans Anderson's Fairy Tales which I still cherish. All the same, I have always felt guilty over winning that prize – had Miss Harvey seen the vest before it was washed, I doubt if I should have won. I very much doubt if she knew much about knitting. She only seemed to teach sewing.

The second prize was for the Schools' Scripture examination. Mother was always quoting passages from the Bible, and all our family regularly attended Sunday School. Consequently I found the examination easy, but all the same, having forgotten all about the examination, I was quite amazed when Mr. Edwards called out my name in the hall as having won a prize – a lovely illustrated New Testament. He signed it with his name, and that I still treasure.

————————THE WAR————————

When the first World War started our class, instead of doing our usual sewing, like pinafores and tea towels, had to stitch sand bags to be used in the trenches in France. Those were terrible times. My brother Stenson was called up at the age of eighteen, and I still recall the telegram arriving from the War Office, saying he had been severely wounded. He was a stretcher bearer in the R.A.M.C. Apparently he had lain all night in the trenches, and in the morning managed to crawl over the shell ridden fields for three miles, before reaching the nearest Casualty Station. A piece of shell was lodged dangerously near his lung, and as a consequence, he was barred from any more Active Service, but continued to serve as an Accountant, in Cardiff, and later on in Perth, Scotland.

Before rationing came into force, Mother was at her wit's end trying to obtain enough food for all her large family. People with small families fared better. As soon as news of any lard, sugar, butter, etc., came over the pipeline, there would be a rush to join the long queues forming outside the shops. It was a case of all hands to the plough, and we children went running all over Knowle, and even down to Slaters, the Pork Butchers, where they made their own lard. Their shop was on the corner of Cheapside and Oxford Street. On hearing that a shop in Wick Road, Brislington had a supply of jam, my younger brother was sent post haste to try his luck. After long queueing, he returned, puffing and panting up Talbot Lane, flourishing a precious pound of jam.

The dreadful 'flu epidemic which raged all over the city added to the misery of those dark days. It was probably made much worse because of the loss of good nourishing food. Many of my schoolfriends died, nearly every surrounding road had its casualties. Mother had five of us in bed at the same time, and we used to dread her appearance when bringing the Fennings Fever Cure bottle. It was really dreadful stuff, bitter as gall, but it evidently cured us. Mother only sent for Dr. Joe Lucas who lived at the bottom of the George Hill, because of my eldest sister needing a certificate for her office. When he came and observed all our wan faces peering at him from under the bedclothes, he remarked: "Well, Mrs. Turner, you seem to have sent for me now that they are all recovering", which made Mother feel rather embarrassed, but one hesitated to call in a doctor in those days because of the cost, especially when five children were involved. However, our doctor's fees were always very reasonable. We all loved his son – young Joe we called him – when he took up practice along by the tram terminus. The house is now occupied by Mrs. Stamper, wife of the late Dr. Stamper. Several years later, when my son was born in 1933, Dr. Old Joe stayed all night at the Hampstead Nursing Home in Hampstead Road, dozing in a chair before I gave birth, and then, instead of going home, climbed up the steep slippery hill leading up to Withleigh Road, in order to inform the family of the new arrival. That was at 6 a.m. He had obviously walked down that way, instead of using his car. He was a very heavily built man, and must have found the climb very exhausting.

Mother had her own ideas about what was appropriate for our various ailments. I seem to remember castor oil and syrup of rhubarb, Parish's Chemical Food for anaemia, from which I suffered, a heated bag filled with hops for earache, but Andrews Liver Salts did nothing to alleviate my frequent attacks of biliousness. Of course there was ipecacuanha wine and Dr. Collis Browne's Chlorodyne, not forgetting a Bella Donna Plaster for back

20

ache. The one unheard of remedy was Aspirin, which would have been a god-send to all of us. My eldest sister suffered terribly from attacks of migraine, not really diagnosed in those days, and she also suffered from nettle rash, when Mother would gather fresh young nettles if available, making nettle tea.

Dr. Joe Lucas used to ride around in those early days in a small horse drawn carriage, with his coachman perched in front. Whenever we had occasion to visit his surgery, it was nothing unusual to see his little white dog lying on the surgery bed wearing a bandage on his paw. Nurse Treble, who lived on the opposite side of the Wells Road, explained that the dog was never happier than when it was pretending to be a patient.

——CHRISTMAS FESTIVITIES——

Christmas and Easter times were always exciting. On Christmas morning the brass band would come round playing carols, and on Good Friday morning we were always awakened very early by the boys shouting: "One a penny, all hot cross buns", and then Father would reluctantly rise from his warm bed, in order to get dressed and buy some.

Preparations for Christmas were almost as exciting as the actual celebrations. The shops of course would be well decorated, and the poultry would be displayed outside Elliott's and Baker's shops. When Mother was preparing the pudding mixture, we all had to stir and make a wish. There were so many things I wanted to wish for – I firmly believed that my particular wish would eventually materialise, but although I am able to remember so many incidents in my early childhood days, I have never remembered if any of my wishes came true. Making the big cake was a long and tedious process. All the fruit was scrupulously washed and dried in front of the fire, then the currants would have to be picked over and – the worst job of all – the raisins would have to be stoned. We always had a cup of water handy in order to rinse our fingers. There were no packets of dried fruit in the shops, already prepared, although Mother would doubtless have still cleaned every currant and every raisin. Then the eggs were finally added, generally about six, especially if she followed a recipe taken from Mrs. Beeton's Cookery Book, which even now still reposes in my bookcase, but I think she often reverted to the recipes she had used in her girlhood days. Then came the beating of the mixture, which had to last for at least twenty minutes. There were no Regulo ovens, so it was a gamble as to whether the correct temperature of the oven was achieved. One unfortunate Christmas, Father inadvertently opened the oven door, probably thinking the gas had been left on with nothing inside. That was a real calamity! When Mother removed the cake, it had sunk in the middle!

Mother was a wonderful cook. She made practically everything, potted meat, meat roll, delicious pork pies made from minced pork steak. Her pastry was always light and flaky – I can still taste the delicious mincepies, lemon tarts and cheese cakes. The present day shops have never produced delicacies of such perfection.

On Christmas Eve I was always too excited to sleep. We four girls slept in our large back bedroom, and I would listen for Father to come creeping along the landing. I doubt if he was aware that one small person was peeping when he filled the stockings hanging on the bed posts. Early on Christmas morning I would wake Chrissie and we would both fumble at the stockings, much to the annoyance of our two elder sisters. The novelty of Christmas was nothing new to them. There was always an apple, an orange, a pink sugar mouse, and a halfpenny at the bottom of the stocking. We never expected much in the way of presents. Although my father had what was considered a responsible position, the Railways in those days were not noted for their generosity towards their employees in the way of salaries. A visit to the Penny Bazaar and the Threepenny and sixpenny Woolworths had to be patronised before the great day. Of course there was no such thing as a Family Allowance in the early nineteen hundreds. Everything had to depend on one's earnings, and feeding, clothing and educating six children did not allow for expensive presents. Still, we all enjoyed opening our presents, and as soon as the fire was lit in the front room, our Christmas Day had begun.

When the wonderful aroma of roast chicken wafted in to us, we knew Mother was preparing the big dinner. On seeing the decapitated bird, baked to a golden brown, I always spared a thought for all the birds whose only Christmas was a pretty deadly one, in the true sense of the word. Still, I always conquered my misgivings, and was soon waiting for the appearance of the Christmas pudding. We knew Mother would have carefully inserted some silver threepenny pieces inside – they were so tiny that one had to be very cautious in tackling one's portion in case we swallowed one.

We always insisted Mother had a rest from the washing up. Sister Marjorie always washed the dishes, while the rest of us would dry them and put them all away. Mother and Father always went upstairs for a rest, whilst we occupied ourselves quietly downstairs. The cake was always iced to perfection and pronounced perfect, and

Mother would beam with pride at all her offspring. In the evening we played games, generally with cards. Speculation played with nuts for money was a favourite one, and we always enjoyed Rummy. Radios of course had not then been invented, but we still had a rip roaring time.

Until we were older, our pocket money consisted of one halfpenny and it was surprising what that one small coin would purchase. Mine was spent immediately, but my sister Chrissie, who always had marvellous will-power, generally saved hers for four weeks, when she would then buy a 2d. bar of Cadbury's chocolate.

There were some quite good shops at the Triangle. Singers sold sweets, and would also take in laundry. Pickards, next door was a dairy, then came the Post Office which was so badly missed when it was finally closed. Hilbornes sold fruit and vegetables, then came the cobbler's shop. We used to go along and watch the shoes and boots being mended, and have a chat with the cobbler. I was always fascinated when he spoke with small nails protruding from his mouth. I was always afraid he would swallow them.

——————CHURCH GOING——————

Harrowdene Church being practically on our doorstep, it was inevitable we should all attend. It was a huge building, containing a large schoolroom with a platform, side rooms and a kitchen and also two toilets, then a door would lead into the Church, which had lovely stained glass windows, a fine pulpit, with the choir stalls behind. The woodwork was light oak in colour, and the pulpit was beautifully carved. The fine gallery was always packed at anniversary times and sometimes important weddings. To help towards reducing the debt incurred when the Church was built, a bazaar was held for three days at the Totterdown Y.M.C.A. hall. The price of admission was three pence, programmes just two pence. The Senior School girls put on the play "Cinderella". Chrissie and I were two of the little fairies, and we also danced the Highland Fling. The Cinderella costumes were exquisite, all made by Mr. Rogers, a tailor. His wife was one of the Beavis Mineral Water Manufacturers family. They played a big part in encouraging the building of Harrowdene Church, also Wells Road Schools.

We always attended church three times on a Sunday. Father would look very impressive in his top hat and Sunday best suit. He was a sidesman, so we were allotted one of the larger back seats.

When the choir filed in, the ladies would divide, altos from sopranos, sister Dorothy was in the alto pew, and all the men sat at the top of the choir stalls alongside the organist, Raddy Wilcox she was called, but I believe her name was Rachael, and afterwards she married the minister, the Rev. Deighton. The organ was worked by someone at the back of the organ pumping vigorously. It was hard work, as I knew to my cost. Brother Alfy used to practice playing on a Saturday afternoon when he had left school, and then Father would pump for him. If he was not available, I used to have a go, but it was a tiring job, and I had to keep resting.

On Saturday evenings, Chrissie and I had our long hair tied up in curl rags, ready for the Sunday parade. The hard knobs of the rags were very uncomfortable at night, but it was all for the sake of beauty! We always looked forward to the Sunday School Christmas parties, and waited with bated breath for our names to be called out by Father Christmas, in order to receive a present from the Christmas Tree. On prize giving day, we always hoped we should like our books. Many of them pointed a moral, but as we grew older,

24

we had a choice, and would carefully look down the lists of books generally advertised in recent books.

We had lovely concerts, arranged by Mrs. Wesley, wife of the choirmaster. All entertainments were popular in those days, before the advent of the Radio and Television, and were well patronised. Latecomers sometimes found difficulty in obtaining a seat, although the Hall was very large. Chrissie and I would go round to Mrs. Wesley's house in Hampden Road, practising to dance the "Highland Fling", also a duet called: "You shan't Play in our Yard". For the duet, we wore pink sunbonnets, blue gingham pinafores, and "stockings of red", as the song went. Mother and sister Dorothy made the clothes, but being unable to purchase red stockings, white ones were dyed. In the song, we were supposed to quarrel, and once I was so carried away with the spirit of the event I gave Chrissie a violent push, nearly knocking her off the platform. Afterwards, she was furious. Another duet was a rather stupid one: "Two Little Sausages". This also entailed a quarrel, but as neither was able to move hand nor foot in our sausage costumes, nothing untoward occurred. Mother once told me that when brother Alfy was in a concert, the audience was convulsed with laughter. As he and the other boys were marching proudly round the platform, he was frantically hanging on to his trousers, which apparently were in grave danger of falling down. Afterwards, on asking Mother why the audience were so amused, he was quite mortified on hearing the reason.

─────── ENTERTAINMENT ───────

We always enjoyed Sunday evenings after Church, when the piano would be in full use. Father would play hymns, singing in his bass voice, whilst Mother's prize piece was "The Maiden's Prayer", also the "Fairy Wedding Waltz", which she always ended with a run up and down the piano keys. As we grew older, Alfy would take over – he learned to play from Miss Oatridge, afterwards becoming Mrs. Budd. She lived in one of the houses at the bottom of the George Hill. Mother and Father were of course Victorians, Father's father being a devout Baptist, always having prayers before breakfast. We always said Grace before our meals until the habit died out, the family being split up with the boys departure to the City School. I am afraid we rather gabbled the Grace: God bless this food which now we take to do us good, for Jesus Christ's sake, Amen". For quite a long time, no sewing, knitting, crocheting or any other activity was

25

allowed on a Sunday, until I think Mother got "fed up", trying to amuse us all, and we were soon happily engaged in our various activities. Eventually, even a game of cards was allowed, just Rummy, Snap, and ultimately, we actually played Whist. In later years, Mother and Father loved to go to the Whist Drives held at the Gaiety Ballroom, also the Cricket Pavilion, where Mother, who was a wizard at remembering every card played, often won a prize. Mr. Martin ran one of the Whist Drives. He lived in Broad Walk. I never cared for card playing, always finding it difficult to concentrate, but I liked a game of Halma, or Crossings, we used to call it, crossing with draughts from one corner of the board to another. Brother Stenson was fond of playing "Fox and the Goose" with draughts. He always tried to rope me into a game, but he defeated me every time.

Although entrance to the cricket field was generally quite free, a charge was made whenever an important cricket match was in progress usually on a Saturday afternoon. We used to have great fun in the field outside the ground, clambering over the piles of telegraph poles stacked by the side of the hedge. Beyond this hedge was another field, reaching up to the back gardens of the Wells Road shops. I believe it was owned by St. Gerard's Catholic Church, because they often had a carnival there, and I can also recollect Father Murphy, a rather stout, ruddy faced priest, very much loved by his community. Once there was a Baby Show held in the field, and it was well patronised by numbers of doting mothers.

One Saturday afternoon, during a cricket match, when one had to pay, Kitty and I were at a "loose end", not knowing where to go. Meeting Chloe Marshall, who lived in Somerset Road, we asked her where she was going. We felt quite envious when she replied she was off to the cricket match, asking us to go along with her, but we had no money. "Don't worry – you can come in with me. My father is a member and I have his membership card", she replied, so feeling rather dubious, we approached the ticket office. She duly showed her membership card, and when he looked towards Kitty and myself waiting for us to offer our money, we nervously stated that we were all sisters. He took a look at us, then waved Chloe into the ground, but refusing to let us in. I do not know to this day why he relented. It could have been my crestfallen expression, but he suddenly changed his mind, and gave us permission to enter. We felt rather sheepish as we walked past the Box, but never tried that trick again.

When a Flower Show was held in the field, formerly the old golf links behind the Cricket Ground, it finished up with organised races. I entered my name, and when it was time for my race to commence, for some reason or another, I was told to station myself a good way

26

down the field. I know I was quite small, but I think we all had to give our ages, and I was the youngest of that group. When the starting whistle blew, away I went, leaving the rest of the field far behind. The organisers had given me too big a start, and I jumped over the rope fixed in front of the tennis courts. All the winners had to go back to the ground in the evening. I was presented with a silver cake dish, not much use to me, but still, it was a prize.

When the Bedminster Hippodrome changed from being a music hall to a cinema, during our summer holidays we were allowed to go as we had no cinema at Knowle. Crossing Victoria Park, we reached Windmill Hill, walking down Fraser Street, and under the railway arch. There was always a horrible smell in Philip Street, which seemed a very poor locality. Parents and children seemed to be sitting on their door steps – they had no front gardens, but it was the smell we objected to most of all. I believe there was a bone factory quite near – either bones or something else which smelt vile.

When the Knowle cinema opened, we decided to try that instead of the Bedminster Stoll Theatre, as it was afterwards called. We were very upset when the usherette directed us to the very front row. That row of seats should never have been allowed. Looking up at the screen, everything was out of proportion, so noticing some empty seats a few rows back, which we knew were priced the same, we sneaked back and occupied them. Unfortunately, the usherette noticed us, and ordered us to go back to the front row again, so we indignantly refused, and marched out of the cinema. When Father heard of all this, he immediately walked all the way down to Bushy Park, and had a flaming row with the Manager, who eventually apologised, allowing us all to go in free the next night.

However, after that incident, we decided that the Bedminster cinema was far superior, and continued to patronise it, in spite of the long walk there and back.

There were plenty of cigarette cards available in our early days, and we always tried to obtain full series of them, exchanging unwanted cards with our friends. Autograph albums were also very popular amongst the girls. Boys would not indulge in such silly female pastimes. Over the years, I have mislaid mine, which was a pity, as now it would have brought back many memories. One of the teachers at Wells Road School was Mr. Calway, and we all hoped he would favour us by painting in our albums. The painting he did in mine was really beautiful, of deep violet pansies, so rich in colour, and almost like velvet in texture. Sister Dorothy has some very interesting items in her old album. The picture I had painted at the age of twelve years looked absolutely awful to me. I probably thought it was quite a good attempt at the time. Two items tickled my fancy. One was a sort of poem, contributed by an Uncle, who was at the time Editor of the *Long Eaton Advertiser*, and always ready for a joke. It ran as follows:

> A fellow feeling makes us wondrous kind (Shakespeare)
> Methinks the poet would have changed his mind
> If standing in a crowd, he chanced to find
> A fellow feeling in his coat behind.

The next contribution is really a gem:

Where to Live (Advt)
In one of the Choicest Localities of Northern France.

To be Let (3 min. from German Trenches) this attractive & Well Built Dug Out, containing 1 Reception kitchen, bedroom & *Up to Date Funk Hole* (4ft. by 3ft.) all modern inconveniences, including gas and water. This desirable Residence stands 1ft. above water level, commanding an excellent view of the enemy trenches. Excellent Shooting (Snipe & Duck). Particulars of the late tenant – Room 6, Base Hospital, Boulogne.

This was accompanied by a drawing of the Dug Out.

This gem was signed by G. Anstey, July 16th, 1916 (an office friend of my sister). In spite of his terrible experiences, he apparently still had a sense of humour, typical of a number of those brave soldiers.

——HOUSEHOLD CHORES——

How we kept warm before the introduction of electricity, and central heating I cannot imagine. We always kept good fires, although Father had a nasty habit of damping down the fire if he thought it was too big (much to Mother's annoyance). When bedtime arrived, Father would fill the copper warming pan with red hot coals from the fire, warming the beds. We also used stone hot water bottles (rubber ones were not then invented) which invariably fell out from the bottom of the beds on to the floor, rousing the whole household.

It must have been all bed and work for Mother. There were no household aids, such as vacuum cleaners and electric irons and washing machines. The woman who helped twice a week, Monday and Thursday, sprinkled salt and tea leaves on to the carpets. This was supposed to prevent the dust rising. Then there were grates to blacklead, brass to clean, and the spoons and forks, together with the silverware on the sideboard. The knives were cleaned on a board with bathbrick. As for wash days, how I hated them! Father would light the fire under the copper, and if he used too many burnt out pieces of coal from the previous day's fire, Mother would moan because she could not get the water to boil. We had what was termed a "Dolly" for the first stage of the washing. The whole contraption made an awful racket. Even after the clothes had been well rotated, they still had to be well rubbed. There was a large bath for rubbing, in case they were not clean enough, Mother was always fastidious, a bowl for blueing and another bowl for the starch. The washing seemed to last all day, and the smell of boiling clothes permeated the air. To crown it all, Monday's meal consisted of cold meat cut from the Sunday joint, potatoes baked in their jackets, pickles and ending up with hateful rice pudding. I was a very finicky eater. Tuesday's "hash", more remains cooked in a casserole, and liberally laced with carrots and onions, etc., really turned me off. I never drank anything but water. Tea, coffee and cocoa I really disliked, although now, as I seem to require more sustenance, I drink tea, but never more than one cup at a time.

After washing day would come ironing day. Everything was done in routine. This involved heating the iron on the gas stove, creating endless journeys backwards and forwards when the iron had to be replaced with a hot one. I often wonder why modern housewives complain of tiredness when they have practically all labour saving devices. In my young days we had no electricity for lighting. No 'fridges – butter had to stand in a basin of cold water in the pantry, and bacon and meat, although covered from the influx of flies, invariably "went off". Eggs would not keep, and there was never any assurance that they were fresh when bought. Candles were carried to light us up to bed, which seemed to cast weird shadows over the staircase.

We once had a woman helper named Polly. She always seemed to us children to be a bit "simple", but she was a willing worker and attacked all her chores with great vigour. When blackleading the firegrate she was so enthusiastic especially if she saw my fascinated gaze, that she would give a quick rub and polish, at the same time shaking her head and giving violent twitches. It got to the point that I had to stop watching her, as I was beginning also to twitch. She always sat at meals with all of the family. Father would politely ask her if she would like another helping perhaps of pudding, and we all knew what she would reply. "Well, I don't mind if I do, if you can spare it". I could see my brother's grinning face at the other side of the table, and then I would be unable to control my giggles. Unfortunately I have always had a tendency to laugh at the wrong moment, and this was my downfall at school. I only had to look at Kitty Belsten to set me off. Miss Harvey often used to exclaim: "Whenever Kitty Belsten is away, Gladys, you always behave". I still laugh at the balloon incident. We both sat in the front seat by the stationery cupboard. Behind the stationery door Kitty was blowing up one of the long zeppelin shaped balloons. I knew if she blew it up too far, it would subside with a loud shrieking wail. The inevitable happened – she blew that balloon up too far, and I can see her look of consternation, and all the class fell about laughing. That was the end of Kitty's balloon, as Miss Harvey confiscated it.

We all enjoyed being in Miss Edward's class, and she had a vivid imagination. One day she solemnly told all the class that if one went out early in the morning there was a possibility of finding a fairy ring. Now why Kitty and I swallowed that yarn I'll never know, but we did go out into the fields as directed, but of course found no fairy rings where the mythical fairies were supposed to hold their nightly revels. We were careful not to let any of our class mates know of our gullibility.

——MORE ENTERTAINMENT——

The swing in our garden was very popular with our friends. My brother Stenson was adept at standing on the seat, whilst the swing was going higher and higher and then he would jump off. My sister Marjorie tried to do the same, but succeeded in breaking her collarbone. Swinging made me feel sick. When the Flower Show was held on the field behind the old Police Station which is now Calcot Road, I had a ride on a chairoplane. It was dreadful. I felt so sick, and I prayed for the blessed thing to stop. Of course, I *was* sick afterwards.

We sometimes had a real magic lantern show, which necessitated the kitchen being darkened, and we would all wait expectantly for Stenson to insert the slides. Some pictures appeared upside down, but we still applauded. He became interested in photography, developing and printing all his own photos. It was a slide camera, which meant we had to sit quite still for a minute before he took the photos. They all turned out very well, but Mother used to get frustrated when she had to grope about in the dark, and also finding the sink filled up with bowls of solution when the slides were being developed.

Whenever one of us had toothache, necessitating a visit to the dentist, Mother always arranged for us to have a poached egg on our return. Our dentist was Mr. Sampson, who lived in Nutgrove Avenue, Bedminster, which entailed a long walk down St. Lukes Road, and right across Victoria Park. I have no idea why we did not patronise a dentist in Knowle. After all, having had a tooth out is bad enough, without having a long walk home afterwards. When

Father escorted me to the surgery, I sat down in the chair, and refused to open my mouth for the dentist's inspection. Nothing on earth would induce me to do so, and eventually he gave me up as a "bad job". Father was not at all very pleased at such a wasted journey, and I sheepishly returned home and to Mother, preparing to poach the usual egg. What happened to that tooth I have no recollection, but I think it must have been a "first" one. My brother Stenson suggested tying a piece of thread round the offending molar, and then attaching the other end of the thread to the door knob. I was quite aware what was in his mind – he would have opened and slammed the door with fiendish glee! I immediately fought shy of that happening. I presume the tooth eventually wriggled loose, as I have no recollection of what happened to it.

I'll never forget losing a piece out of one of my front second teeth. A boy named Donald Chaffey tugged at a rope on which I was standing, trying to get possession of it, and I fell flat on my face. The jagged end of the broken tooth embedded in my lower lip, and I still have the lump it caused. Mother was very upset over my disfigurement.

Our visit to a pantomime at the Prince's Theatre in Park Row was very exciting, especially as it was "Cinderella". We queued outside the ticket office for quite a long time, until the gates leading to the Pit were opened. Then there was a mad rush down the sloping entrance, everyone anxious to obtain a good seat. Being rather small, and the seats rather a long way back, I had to keep standing up, in order to see the stage. So many of the ladies in front of us seemed to be wearing huge hats, quite unconcerned about blocking anyone's view. Jack Pleasance was Buttons, and we all joined with him in singing: "Watching the trains come in", especially the end part: "and when we have watched all the trains come in, we watch all the trains go out". It was very hot and dark in the theatre. People were chewing sweets, some even eating oranges and apples, but it was all wonderful. Then we had the long walk back to Bristol Bridge, in order to catch the Knowle tram.

————AT THE SEASIDE————

When we went to Weston, we always enjoyed watching the Pierrots. They wore baggy white suits, decorated with black bobs, and cone shaped hats. I was always intrigued about the door at the back of the stage, visualising them changing their costumes. There were several rows of iron seats arranged in front, in the hope they would be filled with onlookers, but we all made a rush to bag a seat on the wall. Charlie Goodman was our favourite, and the leader of the show. His favourite song was: "Have a little bit of my wife's cake", and afterwards all the chorus would sing: "We don't like the girls who sit over there, who sit over there, who sit over there, They ought to pay tuppence and take a chair, We don't like the girls who sit over there". It was really a shame the seats were nearly always unoccupied, but most people put something in the collecting box when one of the Pierrots approached the wall.

We always stayed in what was then termed Apartments. Mother would purchase all the necessary food, the landlady then cooking the meals. It really was not much of a holiday for Mother, traipsing round the shops whilst we were digging on the sands, and we always waited expectantly for her to arrive at the beach, often bringing some penny buns, or some fruit.

Everyone travelled by train. There were no 'buses, and Weston was a favourite resort for visitors coming from Birmingham. They never seemed to mind about the tide going out such a long way, and the crowded beach, filled with deck chairs and donkeys. Bath chairs were available on the promenade for elderly ladies, and we always enjoyed a ride on the top deck of the tram, going along to the Old Pier, where we loved looking at the peep show machines, and watching the people shrieking as they had a ride on the water chute.

We always went away for a fortnight's holiday during the summer months. Weston-s-Mare and Burnham-on-Sea were our favourite places, but one year we spent the holiday at Northwick, near Pilning. I should have much preferred going to the seaside especially as the weather was scorching hot. Our nearest watering place was at New Passage, quite hopeless for bathing. I tried my hand at milking a cow, which was not quite so easy as I thought it would be, spent hours sitting on a wall, cuddling General, the big sheep-dog, and also watched with fascination Mr. Kingscot, the owner of the farmhouse in which we stayed chopping up wood. My sister Chrissie decided a 'bike ride would be a welcome change, so I borrowed a 'bike from Olive, the farmer's daughter, whilst Chrissie rode one owned by another of my sisters. We decided to ride to Aust. The sun was shining, the birds were singing, and the cooler air was very refreshing. Then we arrived at a very steep hill. We went whizzing down – it was really exhilarating, until I suddenly realised there were no brakes on my handlebars. I was going faster and faster, and leaving Chrissie far behind. She kept shouting out to me, I began to feel terrified – the hill seemed to go on and on, until sudden it levelled off. Quite accidentally I pressed my left foot down on to the left pedal, and nearly pitched over the handlebars. That blessed 'bike

stopped, and I realised the pedal acted as a brake. Whoever heard of a 'bike with no handlebar brakes? It must have been very ancient.

————SWIMMING CLASSES————

I narrowly escaped from drowning one year at Burnham. The waves were very rough just by the jetty, and I was trying to reach the other members of my family. The waves were too high and too strong, and I was knocked clean off my feet, landing flat under the water, and having no idea how I could get up, being unable to swim. I still remember resignedly thinking my body would be washed up on to the beach eventually, when someone, seeing me under the water, yanked me up, taking me back to my terrified mother who had vainly tried to reach me. I had swallowed a quantity of salt water, and for at least a year afterwards, every time I closed my eyes in bed, I could feel that sea washing over me. I was ten years old at the time, and even now I still shudder with fear when I see high waves.

It was not until the Jubilee Baths opened that I made up my mind to learn to swim – that was in 1937. My son was just a baby, but I was determined he would never suffer such a catastrophe. A Bristol Mothers' Club was formed, with hardly any of the new members able to swim. What fun we had, although we worked hard. We had no proper teacher until we decided to learn Life Saving. I conquered my fear of the water, but however much I tried I could never conquer my fear of diving. It was a case of mind over matter. I knew exactly what I had to do, but always made a mess of it. I envied several of my fellow club members – they did it so easily. In my innermost mind was the nightmare of once seeing my husband's bleeding head as he cracked his head on the bottom of the Tunnel's swimming pool whilst we were holidaying at Ilfracombe. I always went into the water headfirst, as nothing would induce me to jump in. When we played Follow The Leader, Mrs. Ridgers who seemed to have no nerves at all, always played at being the leader. I was always at the end of the line, and when the ones in front of me suddenly dropped down into the water, I hurriedly went in head first. We all felt very nervous and excited when the time came for us to try for our Bronze Life Saving Medals and we all passed. When we decided to try for the Bar to the Bronze, my partner was rather a poor swimmer, but she badly wanted a medal, so I partnered her. On the day of the examination, the snow lay heavily on the ground, and the weather was freezing. To add to my worry, I had an abscess in one ear, which was very painful, but had I failed to turn up at the Baths, my friend would not have been able to take part in the examination. To this day I do not know how I went through with the whole ceremony – swimming down in order to pick up the brick was the worst part. I suffered dreadfully afterwards. My Doctor treated me for two abscesses in the same ear.

On my daughter's insistence I afterwards partly lost my fear of swimming in the sea. Both my children were good swimmers, having taught them myself when they were very young. Branscombe beach in Devon is rather dangerous, as the beach shelves down to the water, and that day the waves were very high. Christine, my daughter told me to dive into the waves, instead of waiting for them to break, but afterwards I had difficulty in getting out of the water, because of the pebbles being washed back down the steep bank, and she had to yank me out.

I appear to be the only one of those club members who still keep up their swimming at the Jubilee Baths. A few of them have joined a Bowling Club, but I shall always maintain swimming keeps me fit, and has enabled my speedier recovery from the various accidents I have had in the past. A frozen shoulder, an impact fracture of the right humerus, and a year ago I sustained a fractured knee cap. When I obtained my A.S.A. certificate in 1984, for swimming two miles, I felt "on top of the world".

READING – AND EXAMINATIONS

As we had no library at Knowle, Father would frequently call in at the Central Library. We were sadly in need of reading matter, but books were not then displayed to the public. It meant browsing through the catalogues, and of course one was unable to judge whether a chosen title heralded an interesting story. Naturally all the family had different tastes. I loved fairy tales, so Father would choose perhaps "The Pink Fairy Book" for me. My older brothers and sisters liked reading, but invariably had very little time to enjoy library books, as they seemed to have so much homework to do. Mother liked detective tales, also books written by Mrs. Henry Wood. Father preferred more intellectual novels. I always longed to possess one of the Christmas Annuals, but one never came my way. I had to be content reading the old "Chatterbox", which had become very tattered over the years. Once when I was recovering from an illness, Winnie Cowley lent me one of her "Playbox" Annuals, and also a model farm. What pleasure I derived from her kind offer! I always made a desperate effort to get hold of the "Gem" and "Magnet" magazines before they were taken up to the porter's Lodge at the City School for my brother Alf, together with the usual parcel of goodies sent by Mother to augment the rather stodgy food. Alf always hated the frequent appearance of pea soup!

A large wooden trunk stood in the back bedroom, crammed full of old "Strand" magazines, which we were never weary of reading. There were serials of E. Nesbit's "The Railway Children", also plenty of Sherlock Holmes stories.

I wonder how many people of my age still remember the gentleman who often boarded a tram at the Three Lamps' stop. He was the very spit of the late Edward the Seventh, not only resembling him facially, but he aped his stately walk, and wore clothes similar to those of the late monarch. He always seemed conscious all eyes were upon him. According to the rumour circulating at that time, his mother was reputed to have been a housemaid at the Palace! Incidentally, when King Edward was the Prince of Wales, he came to Bristol, and in 1873 opened the Race Course at Knowle.

When I finally reached Standard Five, Scholarship time was looming over me. I knew full well I had no hope of passing. Miss Harvey used to sadly shake her head, saying: "If only you could do sums as well as you do composition, Gladys, you would have a good chance of passing". I often wondered why on earth problems were invented. What did it matter how long it took to fill a bath, or to run a certain number of miles in a certain number of minutes! It was all "double dutch" to me, whom the good Lord had not endowed with a mathematical brain. Ability to draw and write stories would not win scholarships. I must have caused a great deal of worry to my family, and always felt very inferior. Mother used to try and console me by saying she had never been able to master problems when she was at school. She attended a private school, and really I did not believe her, as she always seemed to be very quick on the uptake. As for Father, I had seen his old school reports when he finished his education at a High School.

Well, the fatal day arrived. I believe we sat for the examination at Castle Green School. I failed miserably.

As a last resource to obtain an equal education to that enjoyed by my brothers and sisters, my name was entered to sit for a fee paying place at St. George Higher Grade School. Chrissie had already been a pupil there for a year, obtaining a Free Place.

I was so "fed up" with the whole business that I entered the examination room quite resigned towards another failure. To my absolute amazement, I found I was well equal to the task – there were no problems, just plain old decimals, fractions and simple interest sums which I had mastered, composition, and then dictation. I was bound to pass on dictation. Mother had made sure we all would excel at spelling. She used to drill us in spelling. We all used to sit on the couch, in order of age, and always enjoyed it.

I suddenly realised for the first time I was not such a dud after all. I was all set to start a new life!

——————NEW SCHOOL——————

When the day arrived for my first day at my new school I was quite excited. I donned my new straw boater trimmed with a blue ribbon and the picture of an owl in the front, and my lunch box was duly installed in my brand new satchel. I felt quite important, as I set out with Chrissie. I was rather taken aback when I realised how far we had to walk.

We walked all the way down Withleigh Road, carefully negotiating the steep slippery path which ran alongside the Nunnery Grounds. The Nunnery was run by the Roman Catholic Nuns, and was formerly a Reformatory. On reaching the Bath Road, we crossed over to the Tramway Depot, by Arnos Castle, travelled along Whitby Road into Bloomfield Road, taking the path which ran alongside the Co-op Butter Factory. We were only halfway there then, and I began to wonder how much farther we should have to walk. Arriving at the Netham Bridge which spanned the Feeder Canal, we were assailed by a most obnoxious smell issuing from the I.C.I. Chemical Factory. We eventually reached Blackswarth Road, and at long last reached Redfield, and my new school.

The thought of journeying this way every day, also returning, was rather alarming, but I was assured by Chrissie that sometimes when the weather was too bad for walking the whole distance, we could walk down to Bushy Park, catching the Hanham car, which would take us right to the school gates. Later on, in the winter months, we walked down to Temple Meads Station, catching the train to Lawrence Hill, when another long walk was involved.

My new school appeared to be very impressive. All the new girls were inspected in the hall by Head of the girls, Miss Ashworth, who impressed upon us that our hair must always be neatly tied back, and no jewelry must be worn. Only wrist watches were allowed.

On entering my first form, I immediately noticed a large motto. "Whatsoever is worth doing, is worth doing well".

The two Art rooms and the Science Laboratories were right at the top of the building. It meant climbing endless steps. In the basement were the Cookery and the Dressmaking rooms. It always seemed so chilly down there in the winter months. The Dressmaking mistress was Miss Pierce. Obviously she felt the draught when we descended the steps for her lesson. When the last girl arrived she would always call out in stentorian tones: "Shut that door".

I never enjoyed her lessons. Having to use the treadle machine was very nerve racking. Our machine at home was operated by hand, and I invariably pressed the treadle the wrong way, causing the unthreading of the needle, which meant I had to ask Miss Pierce to re-thread it, much to her impatience.

We ate our sandwiches in the hall. There were no facilities for school dinners. I kept my lunch box inside my desk, and often, when feeling peckish, slipped a hand inside the box, taking surreptitious nibbles.

I detested the smell of the Science Labs, but always enjoyed the Art lessons. Miss Langley was my first Gym mistress. She had a habit of staring into space, saying nothing, and we would then all patiently wait for her to come out of her trance.

Our playground was quite small, so we were allowed to spend our recreation in St. George's Park. After lunch, a number of us would sneak down to the lake, hire a boat, which was strictly forbidden, and it was there I learnt to row.

Meanwhile, the 1914–18 war was soon to end. The first Knowle Armistice service was held at the newly built Gaiety Cinema, conducted by the Wesleyan Minister, the Rev. Harvey Field. He was a brilliant young man, and when we sang: "Oh, Valiant Heart", there was hardly a dry eye in the audience. Little did anyone foresee that a few years later we should be involved in another war. Kaiser Wilhelm was deposed, but eventually another tyrant in Germany would take his place.

──────── POST WAR ────────

My days at my new school passed pleasantly enough barring a few ups and downs. In my fourth year I missed several weeks of schooling. My mother was taken to Hospital in order to undergo a serious operation. This necessitated one of the family taking charge of the household affairs, and the obvious choice was myself. My sister Chrissie was ready to take her matriculation examination, and the older ones were employed in offices. Consequently when I at last resumed school lessons, I found it impossible to catch up on the work I had missed. As I only seemed interested in Art, the Headmaster advised my father to send me to the School of Art, the fees saved at St. George would then cover the Art School fees. Nowadays, one can win a place at a polytechnic college and so proceed to carve a career for one's self, but this opportunity was not available in the early part of this century.

I gladly said goodbye to all my friends at St. George, and joyfully set forth on a new life. Some of the pupils at the new school were quite mediocre – not really very talented, and I soon outstripped them, being promoted to the Painting and Life Classes. At midday, several of us walked down to the Art Gallery at the top of Park Street, partaking of a poached egg on toast and a glass of milk at the Café run by the Cadena. I was a very dedicated pupil, thoroughly enjoying the life, but I suppose all good things come to an end. After one very happy year, I was told by my parents I had to leave, because there seemed no likelihood in the near future of my ever earning a living. London was the only place where I could possibly achieve this, so my halcyon days ended quite abruptly. It all seemed so unfair to me when so many of my fellow students were only at the school just to pass the time away, their parents having no shortage of cash. Chrissie afterwards succeeded in obtaining a place at a Teacher Training College in Cheltenham, and although fees had to be paid, her career was a certainty.

For a long time I was quite inconsolable and I seemed to have no future. I was not eligible for decent jobs, so eventually I was enrolled at the Yost School of Commerce sited in the Pithay. My heart was never in my learning to write shorthand and use a typewriter, and none of the following days in an office gave me any pleasure. Still, it was better than doing shop work, where the hours were then very long, and factory work was out of the question.

Tennis was all the rage in my teenage days. There were several Tennis Clubs in Knowle. Apart from the ones flourishing on the Cricket Field, there was a club on the Wesleyan grounds behind the Church, another at the end of Jubilee Road, run by Harrowdene Road Methodist, and one in Lodway Road. Kitty Belsten and I spent practically every fine evening over at the Redcliffe Courts, and I played in several matches. We all enjoyed Saturdays. There was a Refreshment Hut at the entrance to the Ground, where we could quench our thirst with lemonade.

In joining the Redcliffe Club, one was supposed to attend St. Mary Redcliffe Church, so eventually Kitty and I were confirmed. We used to sit right at the back of the nave, unable to hear a word of the sermon, as there were no microphones in those days. After church, we always walked up to Knowle again, in order to join in the

Sunday perambulations along the Wells Road. All the teenagers sauntered along there after church service. We inevitably went to the dances held in the Parish Hall in Guinea Street, walking there and back. The Band was always the same one, smartly dressed in dinner jackets and bow ties. We danced the One Step, Two Step, Fox Trot, and the Waltz. Those popular tunes still stay in my memory. "Barney Google", "The Red Red Robin", "The Naughty Waltz", and later on we learned how to "Charleston", to the tune of "Black Bottom".

Father worked hard on his allotment in Redcatch Lane, originally a corn field and now Redcatch Park. We were thankful for the produce which helped out with our rations. At one time he grew so many kidney beans that neighbours were only too glad to buy some, and the new potatoes, fresh from the ground, were so easy to scrape, and tasted delicious. He was upset at having to part with his plot of land, and eventually took over part of the rough ground situated at the bottom of Withleigh and Lullington Roads. The soil was very heavy, and full of clay. This piece of land has also now been built on, with houses stretching right down to Kensington Park Road.

The aftermath of the war produced thousands of unemployed – a sad sight to see, when the long queues stretched right along Victoria

40

Street hopefully waiting for a chance of employment at the Labour Exchange. The women who had rallied round eager to "do their bit" all returned from the munition factories. Rationing still continued, but life was gradually becoming more normal. Many street hawkers tried to sell their wares at Bushy Park, but Mother always bought something from them, so thankful that she still had her own family intact and safe from any more fighting. My brother Stenson stayed on with the Army as an accountant, preferring not to join the ranks of unemployed, but we were all upset when we knew he would be going to Cairo, Egypt, for a number of years. Mother and Father travelled up to Liverpool to watch the boat sail. The Band played "The Bells of St. Mary's", and Mother always shed a tear afterwards when hearing that tune played.

I suppose it was inevitable that the women who had played such a large part in helping with the war effort should find life had changed quite considerably. They were more independent. One of the first things they did was to have their hair bobbed. I was full of envy, and started to snip little bits off my long hair. Eventually, Chrissie and I were allowed to have side pieces cut, still leaving our plaits. This was better than nothing. They say "constant dripping wears away the stone". I wore Mother down, until she gave in. I was full of excitement walking down to Bushy Park to the hairdresser. I came back waving my shorn plaits to all my friends. Father professed approval at the new hair style, suggesting my elder sisters should follow suit, but it took them a long time to make up their minds. When I used to watch Mother laboriously pinning up her long hair into a bun at the back of her head, I decided that was not for me. Everybody wore hats in those days, even the men, and hats looked ridiculous perched on the top of a bun. Ladies' hats were large and ugly to my mind. Running down to my first School we never bothered to wear one, only on Sundays. No one was ever seen in Church without a hat, except the male generation. Now all the ladies have their hair 'permed, they are reluctant to dislodge their "set", and hats now are very rarely seen in Church. The old Victorians would have been very shocked. Bobby socks had also come into fashion, much to my delight. Out went the black woollen stockings, being replaced with lisle stockings, not even black, and then artificial silk ones, but schoolgirls still had to wear the regulation black ones, and eventually whilst still at school we were allowed to wear short sleeved dresses and blouses.

The first sign of a change in the landscape around Knowle came when I saw the first council house being built behind the Cricket Field, the start of Kingshill Road. No one ever visualised all our surrounding fields being taken over by literally hundreds, all of the

41

same shape and size, making a very monotonous picture. There seemed to be a lack of trees, with the exception of Broad Walk, about the only decent thoroughfare. First we had Knowle Park, then beyond Daventry Road, Knowle West. Many new occupants of the council houses grumbled at being housed next to people who had formerly lived in what were classed slum houses, remarking these outcasts would no doubt keep their coal in their baths! Shops were very few and far between, and people who had formerly lived in congested areas must have found it very difficult to accept their new surroundings.

As the years drifted by, so did Kitty and I drift apart. We were both courting, I married in 1931, and eventually when my son was aged six years, occupied a house in Harrowdene Road.

Meanwhile Hitler was causing great concern, and in 1939 war was declared. At the same time, my old friend Kitty was dying. I was able to see her before she passed away, at the age of thirty four years. She had been a talented pianist, and I felt her loss so much, looking back to our childhood days, and what fun we had had.

WAR AGAIN

Preparations for air raids were quickly put into action. Air raid wardens were appointed, and shelters appeared all over Knowle. The wardens visited each house bringing along the gas masks, which we were instructed to always carry. Blackouts were to be enforced, and I remember my husband making wooden frames to fit over the windows. He also made our own shelter in the garden and when it was finished I thought how gruesome it appeared. It would be like stepping down into a grave. Children were evacuated. I remember a coach load of kiddies arriving at the bottom of Marston Road to pick up a couple of children. I just could not bear the thought of parting with my son. We carried on fairly normally, until one day, on hearing the sirens, I spotted dozens of 'planes in formation flying towards the north of the city. That was when Filton was bombed, causing so many casualties. Up till then, we had not been really alarmed, but on November 24th, which happened to be my Mother's birthday, the siren sounded, and as we were all at that time feeling nervous because of France capitulating, my husband went outside to see if there was danger threatening. He came rushing indoors, saying flares were being dropped at Whitchurch, and quickly hustled us down to the shelter. Then came the awful drumming of 'planes overhead. I was eight months' pregnant, and my great fear was I should go into labour. Everytime we heard the awful whistling noise made by the bombs, we wondered if they would land on our shelter. In the middle of the raid, my husband crawled out of the shelter, going into the house in order to fetch more bedding. It was bitterly cold down in the dug-out. We could hear the loud explosions as the bombs found their targets, and the wardens rushing about, calling to each other.

It seemed an eternity before the welcome "All Clear" siren sounded. We literally crawled out of the shelter, venturing outside into the street. Everyone else seemed to be doing the same thing. What scenes of horror met our eyes! Roofs had vanished, there was a huge crater in the road just outside our house. My son's friend with whom he had been playing only the previous afternoon, was buried, together with the whole of his family under a smouldering heap of rubble, and their neighbours' house had also had a direct hit. Two wardens had gone in to the houses trying to rescue the trapped inhabitants, and they were also killed. The main water supply, electricity and gas had been damaged, the Wells Road was a shambles, and quite impassable for any vehicle. The lovely Wells Road Infant School was no more, just burnt to the ground, much to my son's grief. The Holy Nativity Church was destroyed, apart from the tower which now is still standing above the new building. As for the shops on the Wells Road, many of them had been destroyed. Edmonds toy and stationery premises were completely destroyed. Bucklers, the new Ironmongery shop nearby was also demolished, burying all the occupants underneath the ruins. Luckily the new Post Office, owned by the Reeves family, escaped.

Afterwards we just existed, longing to be able to stay in our beds instead of having to go out to the shelter. On New Year's Eve, when luckily there was no raid, it was time for me to go to the Walker Dunbar Hospital in Clifton. It was snowing quite hard, and all the time we expected another air raid to be announced over the siren. My daughter was born on New Year's Day, and my first question was: "Is she all right?"

With the destruction of their Infants' school, the children had to be sent elsewhere. My son, being in the top class was able to stay with his teacher in a room made available at the Big School, and then afterwards, it meant going down to School Road School, a much older building, and not at all to his liking, but the teaching standards were very good. Eventually his sister attended the Infant School, but it was so much farther to walk. A new building was erected on the site of the lost school, a very ugly building, but of course it was war time, and the powers that be considered there were not enough

43

children left in the area to justify another school. It became an A.R.P. post, and is now an Evening Institute.

The air raids continued, and we were all weary and missing our little luxuries. Clothing coupons, sweet coupons, shortage of everything, and still queues. To make matters worse, we had a robbery. I had taken my baby in her 'pram down to the shops about 9 a.m. calling in at my parents' house before returning home. It was lucky I did not go home straight away, otherwise I should have met the fellow who had broken in. He had climbed up the ladder which we had been asked to leave against the house in case of incendiaries, and stolen the children's saving stamps, my husband's identity card, broken open the gas meter, and stolen other items. He was caught the next day climbing up a ladder in Ravenhill Road, but I felt the house afterwards was unclean. A dreadful feeling. He was also carrying a gun, so I had a narrow escape.

Bedminster suffered a terrible air raid on the Good Friday, killing many people and destroying many houses and churches. We happened to have gone away from Bristol, but we had a shock when arriving home. The hall was swimming in water, and looking upstairs – well, it was impossible to see anything at all. Everywhere was coal black. Apparently incendiaries had fallen on to the roof of the back bedroom, and fortunately the wardens then on duty were able to put out the fire. It was a case of mopping up the water from the water hoses, and trying to bring back daylight to all the upstairs rooms, but we were grateful we suffered no worse damage. I always worried when my husband had to do his spell of fire watching on his work premises in the heart of the city, especially as it involved mounting watch on the roof.

————————BACK TO NORMAL————————

Gradually buses took over from the trams, and we were soon able to ride as far as Whitchurch, instead of alighting at the Red Lion Terminus. As the months slipped by, the air raids decreased, and people were beginning to go about their normal business. The children had a great time playing on the bombed sites, making various "dens" with the help of all the rubble left from the demolished houses.

Shops on the Wells Road were picking up the pieces, and re-opening. Edmonds took over the shop formerly owned by Fields, a tobacconist and sports shop. Mr. Field used to restring our tennis racquets. After the death of Mr. Reeves of the Post Office, which was in a far better position than in previous years, being much larger and kept practically to just Post Office business, Mrs. Reeves left, and the Post Office then re-opened in the original place. Lattys took over Alan Ball's chemist shop. Benges, the Pork Butcher gradually vanished from the scene. When Keens, the Bakers and Confectioners closed down, they were very much missed. Miss Shapland, the Manageress was a great favourite with all the customers.

Schools suddenly changed their status. St. George, Merrywood and Fairfield Schools, under the auspices of Bristol Education Committee, were to be classed as Grammar Schools, much to the indignation of my son's new headmaster. When I went to the first prize giving in the Great Hall, Mr. Garrett was quick at showing his disapproval of all the new Grammar Schools springing up over-night. "There is only one Grammar School in Bristol, and that is the Bristol Grammar School", were his remarks to a packed hall.

When at last the war ended, cars gradually began to appear, but no one was allowed to park in the roads. Chards, the Builders and Coal Merchants in Redcatch Road, were soon inundated with requests for the lock up garages they had erected. One of the nephews lived in the big house facing what was then known as Queensdale Road, but now for some reason, renamed Oakdene Park. One room was used as an office. Eventually this house and the adjoining ones were demolished, being replaced by the Redcatch Garage, and the Broad Walk Shopping Car Parks.

Before owning a motor 'bike, much later on a car, we enjoyed riding our 'bikes into the country, also going as far as Clevedon. My daughter, until she was old enough to ride, would sit in the basket seat behind her father's 'bike. My 'bike happened to have rather large wheels, and being short of stature, I seemed to be perched up very high from the road. As a consequence, when necessary to alight, I was unable to pull into the nearside kerb, but had to take a flying leap, much to my daughter's amusement, who was very fond of shouting out: "Wait for it, Mother's going to jump". The present small 'bikes would have suited me admirably, but I'm quite sure I could never tackle these congested roads.

Meanwhile, the traffic seems to be ever increasing. Old folk like myself are half scared even to cross a road, and car parking in all the neighbouring thoroughfares is getting beyond a joke, especially when so many firms are allowing their employees to park their vans in front of their houses, rather than accommodating them in their own garages. Large vans create a danger in the roads, and take up room needed for private owners. First thing in the mornings, one can reach Bushy Park from the Red Lion Hill much quicker by just walking. It's a nightmare which our predecessors in Knowle would never have envisaged.

Everyone who either attended Harrowdene Road Methodist or lived in its vicinity was inevitably shocked in the nineteen seventies when the Methodist Community ordered its destruction. The Community reasoned that it was not viable having two Methodist Churches in fairly close proximity. Naturally, Knowle United Methodist worshippers were horrified at the thought of losing their church, which was built in 1874, although it did not enjoy half the amenities enjoyed by Harrowdene. The workmen who had the unenvious task of starting to pull down such a beautiful building confessed they hardly knew where to start. It was in perfect condition, and a landmark for everyone walking up Greenmore Road. So much dedication and love had gone into its structure, just watching the smashing of the lovely stained glass windows and tearing down the elegant pulpit and choir stalls created much sorrow and indignation. To make matters worse, the new houses built on the site in no way conform to the type of houses erected in Cleeve Road at the early start of the century. Certainly the planning authority which allowed them to be built has much to answer for. When the houses in Marston Road were "blitzed", their replacements were exactly in line with the rest of the houses.

—————MORE MEMORIES—————

Many of us who have always known her, miss seeing Mrs. Lott, who once kept the sweet shop at the top of Greenmore Road. The shop in my young days was owned by Brinkworths, afterwards taken over by Mrs. Winnett, who promptly called it "The Local". Mrs. Lott eventually acquired the shop, and after the early death of her husband, carried on also bringing up her daughter Sybil. Sadly, through old age, she has now become housebound. Mrs. Gay, of the former fruit and flower shop, which we all miss so very much, always refers to her as "Queen Victoria".

Many old Knowlites will probably remember Mrs. Venn, who once lived in Sydenham Road. She was a real animal lover, and what she did not know about animal ailments was not worth knowing. Even Dr. Lucas often consulted her, as he was an animal lover.

Care and love of "all creatures great and small" has always been one of my priorities, and I have never hesitated in reporting suspected cases of cruelty to the R.S.P.C.A. An old friend of mine, who once lived on the corner of Maxse Road but sadly died through heart trouble, always used to assert that ignoring cruelty to any dumb animal or bird, just doing nothing about it, means one is condoning it. People have sometimes remarked to me that too much priority is given to animals. I always point out to them that a tender heart to animals also includes a tender heart to humanity. When I read of the badger hunting, hare coursing, cock fighting, and abandoned dogs and cats, I sometimes think Britain has not much improved since the ignorance and callousness of medieval days.

The dreadful winter we experienced in the seventies will always stay in my mind. I hate snow, because I immediately think of the wild creatures cut off from their natural food. I always kept a sharp eye for little sparrows collapsing through the severe cold of that year, and rescued many which had fallen down, too weak and frozen to fly, bringing them in to the warm fire, until they regained their strength. When the great thaw came, I decided to take a walk into Redcatch Park, where I had previously always exercised my beloved collie, who died just before I lost my husband. I dreaded what I should discover in the Park, as hundreds of birds must have died. I certainly saw many pitiful corpses, but what upset me more than ever was seeing two carrion crows pecking at a white object in the distance. When I approached, they immediately flew off, and then I saw their victim. One eye had been completely pecked out of the helpless seagull. Its heart was still beating, but no one else was in the Park, so I gathered it up into my hands, taking it along to the Park Keeper's Lodge. I wordlessly handed it over to the Park Ranger, to be humanely destroyed.

On hearing about the modernising of my children's old Knowle Junior Mixed School, I decided to have a look at all the improvements made. The entrance is now in Cemetery Road, the School Road one now closed. I found it hard to recognise the old building as I had known it when I so much enjoyed the Social evenings, Whist Drives, etc., arranged by the Parent Teachers' Association. The teaching staff was very dedicated to the school and the children, and were to be admired for the dedication they showed, and for giving up so much of their spare time. Strolling back along Cemetery Road, I noticed the neglected garden and old stable which was formerly owned by Dr. Lucas. Hoskins, the furnishing shop, now has taken over.

I sometimes find it hard to realise I have lived in Knowle for nearly eighty one years. Sadly, Knowle, like other Bristol suburbs, will never regain the peace and tranquillity of former days. The serenity has completely vanished. The elegant houses seem to be taken over as bed-sitters and flats. Perhaps it is as well my parents did not live to see so many alterations. They were able to watch the radio, but never saw television. Father enjoyed playing bowls on the Knowle Park Bowling ground, and also took part in a game of solo whist in the Elderly Peoples Club, next door to the Library.

Knowlites have now become reconciled to losing so many of their favourite shops, but one shop has been missed more than any other, Kemble Williams, the large drapery. In the previous years, we had enjoyed the services of two draperies, Tuckfields, who occupied the premises at the bottom of Greenmore, afterwards taken over by the Co-op Grocery, followed by the Butchery, and now by Farrows, the Furniture Store. Kemble Williams took over from Partridges. They improved the shop, extending it at the rear, making it much lighter. I can still recall the few stairs we had to mount in order to reach the wool and corset counters. Losing Harris & Tozers was the final blow.

We feel we are lucky in having the Broad Walk Shopping Centre, and although we miss the personal touch of the small shops, find shopping there much more convenient. In the winter, we breathe the warm atmosphere as we walk in from the outside cold, and appreciate the opportunity of resting on the precinct seats and meeting so many old friends in order to have a chat.

Writing this saga of my early days in Knowle has brought back many memories, which I thought were long forgotten. Experiencing the trauma of two world wars was far from pleasant, and the very thought of another fills me with horror. I still recall the bewilderment I felt on hearing for the first time that war had started in 1914. Everyone seemed to think it would be over by Christmas – how wrong they were!

The trees which were saplings when my parents first arrived in Knowle have now grown to a great height, making a glorious picture when in full bloom, but it behoves the elderly and shortsighted folk to be wary of the huge amount of falling leaves in the Autumn months, making walking over the uneven pavements very dangerous.

My son and I have now moved to a much quieter part of Knowle, where we are entranced by the panoramic view of the glittering City lights and the illuminated Suspension Bridge. I look back once again on those quiet happy days of my youth, when Kitty and I used to run down the grassy slopes which became Perrett's Park given to the community by Alderman Perrett. I still recall him.